The Word Sincerity and Attainment its Meaning

Ibn Rajab Al Hanbali

Translated & Comments by Al Reshah

Alreshah.net

Canada

Alreshah
www.Alreshah.net

Publisher's Note: This is translation of book without change of meaning as best as the translator could achieve with few comments in the footnote to clarify If any error is found please contact us through our website alreshah.net.

Book Layout © 2017 BookDesignTemplates.com

The Word Sincerity and Attainment its Meaning / Ibn Rajab Al Hanbali. -- 1st ed.
ISBN 978-0-9936697-3-6

Thanks for:
Stacey Con
Dawn Birdsong Vadbunker
Fox Buck

For their input and review of this Translation

Footnotes: Mohmmad Ahmad

Contents

The start of the book 1

The benefits of There is no God but Allah. 31

CHAPTER 1

The start of the book[1]

In Sahih Bukhari and Sahih[2] Muslim Reported by Anas (May Allah be pleased with him) Mu'adh was riding on the beast with the Prophet (peace and blessing be upon him), when he (peace and blessing be upon him) said to him, "O Mu'adh!" Mu'adh replied, "Here I am responding to you, and at your pleasure, O Messenger of Allah." He (peace and blessing be upon him) again called out, "O Mu'adh." He (again) replied, "Here I am responding your call, and at your pleasure. Upon this he the Prophet (peace and blessing be upon him) said, "If anyone testifies that there is no true god except Allah, and Muhammad is His slave and Messenger, Allah will safeguard him from Hell." He (Mu'adh) said, "O Messenger of Allah, shall I not then inform people of it, so that they may have glad tidings." He (peace and blessing be upon him) replied, "Then they will rely

---

[1] There is no title for this chapter
[2] Sahih Muslim and Bukhari, are two of the Kutub al-Sittah (six major hadith collections).

on it alone (and thus give up good works altogether)." Mu'adh (May Allah be pleased with him) disclosed this Hadith at the time of his death, to avoid sinning for concealing.

In Sahih Bukhari and Sahih Muslim 'Itban bin Malik (May Allah be pleased with him) reported that the prophet (peace be upon him) said: "Allah has made the fire of Hell unlawful for him who affirms that none has the right to be worshipped but Allah."

In Sahih Bukhari and Sahih Muslim, it is narrated either on the authority of Abu Huraira or that of Abu Sa'id Khudri. with a little bit of doubt, He (the narrator) said: During the time of Tabuk expedition, the (provisions) ran short and the men (of the army) (the narrator) said: He Messenger of Allah (peace and blessing be upon him) called for a leather mat to be used as a table cloth and spread it out. Then he called people along with the remaining portions of their provisions. He (the narrator) said: Someone was coming with handful of mote, another was coming with a handful of dates, still another was coming with a portion of bread, till small quantities of these things were collected on the table cloth. He (the narrator said): Then the messenger of Allah invoked blessing on them and said: Fill your utensils with these provisions. He (the narrator) said: They filled their vessel to the brim with them, and no one amongst the army was left even with a single empty vessel. He (the narrator) said: They ate to their fill, and there was still a surplus. Upon this the Messenger of Allah (peace and blessing be upon him) remarked:

I bear testimony that there is no God, but Allah and I am the messenger of Allah. The man who meets his Lord without harboring any doubt about these two (truths) would never be kept away from Paradise.

In Sahih Bukhari and Sahih Muslim, narrated by Abu Tharr (May Allah be pleased with him) Messenger of Allah (peace and blessing be upon him) said, He said, "Nobody says: 'None has the right to be worshipped but Allah' and then later on he dies while believing in that, except that he will enter Paradise." I said, "Even if he had committed illegal sexual intercourse and theft?" He said. 'Even if he had committed illegal sexual intercourse and theft." I said, "Even if he had committed illegal sexual intercourse and theft?" he repeated this three times, He said. 'Even if he had committed illegal sexual intercourse and theft." For the fourth time I said, 'Even if he had committed illegal sexual intercourse and theft?', in spite of the Abu Tharr's dislike. Abu Tharr said,

In Sahih Muslim, 'Ubadah bin Al-Samit (May Allah be pleased with him) reported: while he was near death. I heard the Messenger of Allah (peace and blessing be upon him) says: "Whoever testifies That There is no true god except Allah and that Muhammad is the Messenger of Allah, then Allah has forbidden the fire for him".

In Sahih Muslim, 'Ubadah bin As-Samit (May Allah be pleased with him) reported at the time of his death, I heard Messenger of Allah (peace and blessing be upon him) says, "He who bears witness that there is no true god except Allah, alone having no partner with Him, that Muhammad is His slave and His Messenger, that 'Isa (Jesus) is His slave and Messenger and he (Jesus) is His Word which He communicated to Maryam (Mary) and His spirit which He sent to her, that Jannah is true and Hell is true; Allah will make him enter Jannah accepting whatever deeds he accomplished".

In this sense, there are many hadiths that are long to be mentioned. The hadiths of this chapter are two types. One of them is that whoever said the two testimonies entered Paradise and did not prevented from it. This is apparent as no one will be abided in fire from pure monotheism people and he may enter Paradise and won't be prevented from it if he purifies his sins in fire.

And the hadith of Abu Tharr means that adultery and theft do not prevent entering Paradise with Tawheed[3] (monotheism) and this is right that has no doubt in it.   It is not in that there is no punishment for them with Tawheed, and in Musnad Al-Bazzar reported by Abu Hurayrah (may Allah be pleased with him) He said: Whoever says, "There is no god but Allah, it benefits him one day, whatever calamity, he is afflicted with it before that.

The second is that he is forbidden to the fire, and this is what some of them have explained it the immortality in fire where its

[3]Tawheed in Arabic means attributing Oneness to Allah and describing Him as being One and Unique, with no partner or peer in His Essence and Attributes.

people eternalize. And it is except the highest depth where a lot of disobedient ones enter because of their sins, and then they go out with the intercession of the defenseless and the mercy of the merciful.

In Sahih Bukhari and Sahih Muslim, that Allah, the Exalted, says: " but by My Honor, Glory, Greatness and Might, I would certainly take him out of fire who professed it: There is no god but Allah".

A group of scholars said that the meaning from these Hadiths is that there is no god, but Allah is the reason to enter Paradise and to escape from the Fire, but it is obligatory for that, and it is required to do this work only by summoning its conditions and avoiding its prohibitions. And this is the saying of Al Hassan and Wahb Ibn Monabeh, and this is the most revealed.

Al-Hasan told Al-Farzadeq while he was burying his wife, what did you prepare for this day. He said that I have prepared "There is no God but Allah" Seventy years ago, Al-Hasan said: this is the best preparation, but "There is no God but Allah" has conditions. Don't do slandering chaste women, it was said to Al Hassan that some people say whoever says There is no God, but Allah enter Paradise, he (Al Hassan) said any one who says There is no God but Allah and do its rights and obligations enters the Paradise.

Wahab bin Munabbih: told anyone who asked him: Is not " there no God but Allah", is the key to Paradise? He said: Yes, but there is no key except for its teeth. If you bring with a key with its teeth, it will be opened for you, otherwise it will not be opened.

In this Hadith that the key to Paradise is "there is no God but Allah" by Imam Ahmad with A broken attache.

Reported by Mu'adh said: The messenger of Allah (peace and blessings be upon him told me, if the people of Yemen asked you about the key of Paradise, say it is the testifying that there is no God but Allah. And what proves this truth is that the messenger peace and blessings be upon him ordered entering the Paradise depending on the good deeds in a lot of texts.

As in Sahih Bukhari and Sahih Muslim, Abu Ayyub reported: A man said to Messenger of Allah (peace and blessings be upon him), "Direct me to a deed which will admit me to Jannah ". The Messenger of Allah (peace and blessings be upon him) said, "Worship Allah and associate no partner with Him, perform As-Salat, pay Zakat, and maintain the ties of kinship"

In Sahih Muslim, Abu Hurairah reported: A man said:"O Messenger of Allah! Direct me to a deed by which I may be entitled to enter Jannah." The Prophet (ﷺ) said, "Worship Allah, and never associate anything with Him, establish Salat, pay the Zakat which has been enjoined upon you, and observe fasting of Ramadan." He (the man) said: "By Him in Whose Hand my soul is, I will never add anything to these (obligations)." When he turned his back, the Prophet (ﷺ) said,

"He who wants to see a man from the dwellers of Jannah, let him look at this man."

And in the Musnad[4] from Basheer ibn al-Khasasiyah, he said: "I came to the Prophet (peace and blessings be upon him) to pledge allegiance to him, he gave me the conditions, that are to bear witness that there is no God but Allah and that Muhammad is his Slave and Messenger; performing prayer; the payment of Zakat; performing Hajj (pilgrimage) the obligatory for Islam, fasting during the month of Ramadan. Striving (Jihad) in the way of Allah. So, I said: Oh, Messenger of Allah I can't bear two of them that are Jihad and Charity.

And they claimed that who turns his back deserves the anger of Allah, I am afraid that if I do this, I liked myself and I hated the death and charity, I swear by Allah I have only a booty and ten camels they and what they hold are for my family, so The Messenger of Allah (peace and blessings of Allah be upon him) grabbed his hand and then moved it. Then he said: "There is no jihad and no charity, then how can you enter the paradise" so I said Oh messenger of Allah I pledge allegiance to you, I pledge allegiance for all of them.

In this hadeeth, jihad and charity are condition for entering Paradise with monotheism (Tawheed), prayer, fasting and Hajj. And what equals this is that the Prophet (peace and blessings of Allah be upon him) said: "I have been ordered to fight people

---

[4] Hadith in Musnad Imam Ahmad

until they testify that there is no god, but Allah and that Muhammad is the Messenger of Allah"[5]. So, Omar and a group of companions understood that whoever testifies the two testifyings is stopped from being punished in life because of this, so they stopped fighting that who doesn't pay Zakat. Al Sediq[6] realized that they will not be fought if they do its rights.

As the Messenger (peace and blessings of Allah be upon him) said that if they did then their blood will be protected from me, except what it makes obligatory upon them, and their reckoning is up to Allah."

And he said: "Zakat is the right of money, and this is what Al Sediq has understood." Narrated by Al-Sediq on the authority of the Prophet, peace and blessings of Allah be upon him, more than one from companions narrated it, including Ibn 'Umar , Annas and others. [7]

---

[5] Note: this Hadith is part of Jihad overview in Islam and should not be taken out of the context of rules of Jihad in Islam and ignore the underlying Fact in Islam which as stated in Quran " There shall be no compulsion in [acceptance of] the religion." 2:256 or "And if they incline to peace, then incline to it [also] and rely upon Allah. Indeed, it is He who is the Hearing, the Knowing. "8:61 etc. , the Author here didn't expand on this subject as in the same way he didn't expand on Fasting rules nor prayer times and requirement nor Zakat ratio and limits. Because simply this is not the theme of the Book as his aim here is to link deeds as a requirement of Tawheed. And not explain deed itself, so if a person wants to know more about Rules of Jihad, Fasting or Prayer better to look for a book cover those subject in detail and not take this Hadith out of it is context.

[6] Abū Bakr aṣ-Ṣiddīq 'Abdallāh bin Abī Quḥāfah the first Muslim Caliph following Muhammad's (peace and blessings of Allah be upon him) death

[7] In different Hadith books " Abu Hurairah (May Allah be pleased with him)

Also the Messenger of Allah (peace and blessings of Allah be upon him) said, "I have been commanded (by Allah) to fight people until they testify that there is no true God except Allah, and that Muhammad is the Messenger of Allah, and perform Salat and pay Zakat, it is clear from Allah the most high says " إن تَابُوا وَأقامُوا الصَّلاة وآتُوا الزَّكاة فَخَلُّوا سَبِيلَهُمْ"8, But if they repent and perform As-Salat (Iqamat-as-Salat), and give Zakat, then leave their way free"

regarding the saying of Allah the Most High: "فإن تَابُوا وأقامُوا الصَّلاة وآتُوا الزَّكاة فإخوانُكُم في الدِّين9 "But if they repent and establish worship and pay the poor due, then are they your brethren in religion.

---

reported:

When the Messenger of Allah (ﷺ) passed away, Abu Bakr (May Allah be pleased with him) was appointed as his successor (caliph). Amongst the Arabs some men apostatised. Abu Bakr (May Allah be pleased with him) resolved to fight them. 'Umar bin Al-Khattab (May Allah be pleased with him) said to Abu Bakr: "How can you fight them when the Messenger of Allah (ﷺ) has declared: 'I have been commanded to fight people till they testify La ilaha illallah (there is no true god except Allah); and if they do it, their blood (life) and property are secured except when justified by law, and it is for Allah to call them to account." Upon this Abu Bakr (May Allah be pleased with him) said: "By Allah, I would definitely fight him who makes distinction between Salat and the Zakat, because it is an obligation upon the rich to pay Zakat. By Allah I will fight them even to secure the piece of rope which they used to give to the Messenger of Allah (ﷺ)." 'Umar (May Allah be pleased with him) said: "I realized that Allah opened the heart of Abu Bakr (May Allah be pleased with him) for fighting those who refused to pay Zakat, and I fully recognized that Abu Bakr

8 At-Tawba 9:5
9 At-Tawba 9:11

The brotherhood in religion is not proven except by the performance of obligatory duties with Tawheed (monotheism). Repentance from shirk does not take place except in Tawhid (monotheism). When Abu Bakr proved this to his companions, they returned to his saying and realized that it is right.

If it is known that the punishment in life does not stopped totally for the person who testified the two testifyings, but he is punished by violating one right of the rights of Islam, so the punishment of the Hereafter has the same way in punishment.

A group said that the first Hadiths mentioned, and their meaning were before the descent of obligations and limits, this group such as Al Zahri, Al Thawri and others. And this is very far as many of them were in Al Madeena after the descent of obligations and limits and in some others that he was in Battle of Tabuk, and it is in the last life of the Prophet peace be upon him, and some of them say that those Hadith are abrogated and some of them say that these are valid, but they added conditions and this indicated that the addition of the text is abrogation or not , the dispute in this is among fundamentalists is famous, Al Thawri and others stated that they are abrogated and obligations and limits has abrogated them, they may intend by abrogation is explaining and interpretation. The ancestors used to call this abrogation on thing like this a lot, their intention is that the verses of the obligations and limits indicate that entering Paradise and the escape from the fire depend on doing obligatory duties and avoidance of unlawful acts.

These texts were abrogated that means they are explanatory text and the texts of limits and obligations are abrogating (the previous ones) that means explaining the meanings elaborating them.

Another group said that these free texts have been restricted in other Hadiths, in some of them whoever says there is not God but Allah sincerely, in others being whole-heartedly, in others his tongue believes, in others he says it truly from his heart, in others his tongue humbled to it and his heart trusted to it.

This is all a reference to the work of the heart and its verification in the sense of the two testifying, to achieve it by saying that there is no God but Allah, that the heart doesn't have any other God, due to love, hope, fear, confidence, seeking support, obedience, repentance, asking, and fulfilling that Muhammad is the Messenger of Allah. And not to worship anyone other than what Allah has decreed on the tongue of Muhammad (peace and blessings of Allah be upon him) This meaning came to the Prophet (peace and blessings of Allah be upon him) who said explicitly: "Whoever says that there is no God, but Allah sincerely will enter Paradise." It was said: "What is its sincere? O Messenger of Allah." He said that you should be prohibited from what Allah has forbidden you. This is narrated from the Hadith of Anas ibn Malik and Zaid ibn Arqam.

But their attribution is not valid, also it came from Al-Hasan in the same way.

Achieving this meaning and explaining it, is that the saying of the servavt that there is no God but Allah. And the God is the one who is obeyed and doesn't disobeyed due to his prestige, reverence, love, fear and hope, asking him, praying for him and this is not fit at all but to Allah Almighty.

Anyone who involves any creature in one of these things, which are characteristics of the godlike, was abuse to his sincerity in saying that there is no god but Allah. And this is lack of his monotheism and it was the slavery of the creature according to what in it, and all of this is branches of polytheism (Shirk) and this is why it is called polytheism, because of the sins that arise from not being obedience to Allah, or feeling his fear, his hope, confidence, or trust in him and work for him as stated in the calling of polytheism on hypocrisy and for swearing by anyone or anything other than Allah and on trusting other than Allah and relying on him.

And also, who made equals the Allah and creature in the will, such as to say What Allah wills and so-and-so wills'[10], but say: 'What Allah wills, and then what so-and-so wills." Also, his saying I depend on Allah and you,

---

[10] It have same meaning to Sahih Hadith mentioned in Sunan Abi Dawud **Narrated Hudhayfah:**

The Prophet (ﷺ) said: Do not say: "What Allah wills and so and so wills," but say: "What Allah wills and afterwards so and so wills.

As well as what slanders in the monotheism (Tawhid) and the uniqueness of Allah for benefiting and harming, such as evil omen and hated charm and going to kahins (fortunetellers) and believe them in what they say as well as following the passion of self in what Allah has forbidden, in what slandering perfection of tawhid and its integrity.

This is why the Sharia has named many of the sins that originate from the desire of the soul polytheism and unbelief such as fighting Muslim, 'Whoever has intercourse with a menstruating woman, or with a woman in her rear, and drink wine at the fourth time [1], although this does not let him be out of sect , this is why the salaf said that one disbelief is different from other disbelief and shirk is different from shirk.

It is mentioned that the revelation of God for the followed desire, Allah the most high says [12]"أَفَرَأَيْتَ مَنِ اتَّخَذَ إِلَهَهُ هَوَاهُ" Have you seen he who has taken as his God his [own] desire, is that whatever he like something he follows it, Qotada says that is the one who whenever he likes something, he follows it.

And whenever he wishes something he does it, nothing can prevent him from doing so such as God-fearing or pious. It is narrated from Abu Amamah Hadith with a weak attribution.

---

[11] Note by Imam al-Albani in his book related to the same title that this addition of "he don't know a hadith which call shirk or kufr on whom drink wine for the fourth time "
[12] Al-Jathiya 45:23

There is   nothing under the sky, worse than the sin of worshiping a god other than Allah like following a passion, and in another Hadith that " There is no God but Allah benefits who believe in it until they prefer their life to their religion, if they do this, it will be against them and they are told that you have lied,[13] and it is ensured by Hadith sahih of the Prophet (peace and blessings of Allah be upon him "Wretched is the slave of the Dinar, the slave of the Dirham and the slave of the Khamisah. He is wretched and will be thrown (into Hell) on his face, and if he is pricked with a thorn may find no relief."

This indicated that that everyone who loved something and obeyed it, and it is his goal and desire, and he was loyal for it, then he is its slave and that thing is his idol and his God, also what indicates that is that Allah the most high called the obedience of Satan in his disobedience worship of Satan as he said, "أَلَمْ أَعْهَدْ إِلَيْكُمْ يَا بَنِي آدَمَ أَن لَّا تَعْبُدُوا الشَّيْطَانَ"[14] "Did I not enjoin on you, O ye Children of Adam, that ye should not worship Satan".

And Allah the most high says about his friend Abraham, May Allah be pleased with him   said to his father, "يَا أَبَتِ لَا تَعْبُدِ الشَّيْطَانَ إِنَّ الشَّيْطَانَ كَانَ لِلرَّحْمَٰنِ عَصِيًّا"[15]"O my father! serve not Satan: for Satan is a rebel against (Allah) Most Gracious." , anyone who did not achieve the slavery of Rahman and obey him, he worships Satan by his obedience to him, and no one will get rid

[13] Note by Imam Al-Albani this Hadith is not Valid
[14] Ya-Sin 36:60
[15] Maryam 19:44

from Satan worship except who are sincerely worship Allah the merciful.

And they are the ones who Allah said about them " إنَّ عِبَادِي " لَيْسَ لكَ عَلَيْهِمْ سُلْطَانٌ [16] Except, among them, Your chosen servants." Those are who understood the word there is no God but Allah, they are matching their words by their deeds. So, they will not turn away from Allah because of love, wish, fear, obedience, and confidence.

They are honest in saying that there is no God but Allah, and they are the true servants of Allah, but whoever says that there is no God but Allah only by his tongue, and then he obeys the Satan and his desires in disobeying Allah and his transgression. He has lied to his deeds, saying that there is a lack of perfection in as much as disobeying Allah in obedience to the Satan and desire. [17] " وَمَنْ أَضَلُّ مِمَّنَ اتَّبَعَ هَوَاهُ بِغَيْرِ هُدًى مِنَ اللَّهِ " "And who is more astray than one who follows his desire without guidance from Allah" don't follow your desire. And this will lead you away from the path of Allah,

Oh, you be servant to Allah not servant to desire, surly the desire ends its follower to fire. [18]" أَرْبَابٌ مُتَفَرِّقُونَ خَيْرٌ أَم اللَّهُ الْوَاحِدُ الْقَهَّارُ " are separate lords better or Allah, the One, the Prevailing , "May he be miserable, the worshipper of the dinar and dirham, By Allah, no one will be saved tomorrow from Allah's punishment only if he achieved worshiping Allah alone, and not to look to

---

[16] Al-Hijr 15:24
[17] Al-Qasas 28:50
[18] Yusuf 12:39

any other else, anyone who knows that Allah is one to be worshipped and not to have any partner in worshipping him.

Some of the knowledgeable people were speaking to his companions on the top of a mountain, and he said in his words that no one will reach his goal until he worships Allah alone.

He was disturbed and upset until his companions saw that the rocks had been hardened and he remained for an hour. When he woke up, it was as if he had resurrected from his grave.

 The Saying that there is no God, but Allah requires that the one does not love anyone else but Allah. The God is the one who is obeyed. He does not being disobeyed because of love, fear and hope. And the perfection of his love is to love anything that he loves and dislike what he dislikes. Anyone who likes anything that Allah dislike or dislikes anything that Allah likes, his monotheism and belief for saying there is no God, but Allah is not complete, and he has a hidden shirk according to what he dislikes from what God loves and loves what God dislikes. Allah the most high says[19] ' ذَلِكَ بِأَنَّهُمُ اتَّبَعُوا مَا أَسْخَطَ اللَّهَ وَكَرِهُوا رِضْوَانَهُ فَأَحْبَطَ أَعْمَالَهُمْ " That is because they followed what angered Allah and disliked [what earns] His pleasure, so He rendered worthless their deeds. Al Laith narrated from Mujahid his saying that they don't associate with me anything said they don't love other than me.

---

[19] Muhammad 47:28

In Saheeh al-Hakim from 'Aa'ishah (may Allah be pleased with her), the Prophet (peace and blessings of Allah be upon him) said: "The shirk in this nation is hidden from the slowly movement of ants on the rock at the dark night, and its minimum is that you love something that is unfair or hate something of justice. Isn't religion only the love and hate.

Allah, the Exalted, says [20] "قُلْ إِن كُنتُمْ تُحِبُّونَ اللّهَ فَاتَّبِعُونِي يُحْبِبْكُمُ اللّهُ" Say: "If ye do love Allah, Follow me: Allah will love you, and this is a text that shows the love of what Allah dislikes and dislikes what he likes is following the desire and continue to do so and counteracting it is from the hidden shirk. Al Hassan says that you should know that you will not love Allah until you love his obedience. Tha Al Noon was asked when I love my lord? He said if what he dislikes is more bitter than aloes.

Ibn Besher Al Sori said it is not of the marks of love to love what your lover dislikes,

Abu Yacoub al-Nahr said that all those who claimed the love, and don't match this to his deeds, his claim is not valid. Yahya ibn Mu'adh said, "He is not a believer who claimed the love of Allah and did not keep his limits." Ru'im said: "Love is the matching in all cases, and he sang ... If you say to me die, I will obey, and I say to the callers of death, "Hello and welcome".

And what attest to this meaning also is the saying of Allah the most high:[21]" قُلْ إِنْ كُنْتُمْ تُحِبُّونَ اللَّهَ فَاتَّـبِعُونِي يُحْبِبْكُمُ اللَّهُ " "If you should love Allah, then follow me, [so] Allah will love you, "

---

[20] Al-i-Imran 3:31
[21] Al-i-Imran 3:31

Al-Hasan said," The companions of the Messenger of Allah (peace and blessings of Allah be upon him) said: 'We love our Lord very much, so Allah liked to have a mark for his love, so Allah revealed this verse. From here, it is known that the witness of there is no God, but Allah is not complete without witnessing that Mohammad is Allah's messenger.

If it is known that the love of Allah is only complete with loving what he loves and hating what he hates, there is no way to know what he loves and hates except by Muhammad who reports from Allah what he loves and what he hates by following what he ordered and avoiding what he forbade. So, the love of Allah is required to the love of His Prophet (peace and blessings be upon him) and believing and following him up. for this reason Allah matches between his love and the love of His Messenger in his saying the most high: " قُلْ إِن كَانَ آبَاؤُكُمْ وَأَبْنَاؤُكُمْ وَإِخْوَانُكُمْ وَأَزْوَاجُكُمْ وَعَشِيرَتُكُمْ وَأَمْوَالٌ اقْتَرَفْتُمُوهَا وَتِجَارَةٌ تَخْشَوْنَ كَسَادَهَا وَمَسَاكِنُ تَرْضَوْنَهَا أَحَبَّ إِلَيْكُم مِّنَ اللّهِ وَرَسُولِهِ" [22]

Say, [O Muhammad], "If your fathers, your sons, your brothers, your wives, your relatives, wealth which you have obtained, commerce wherein you fear decline, and dwellings with which you are pleased are more beloved to you than Allah and His Messenger.

Also, he associated his obedience and his messenger (peace and blessings be upon him) obedience together in many places, the messenger said "Whoever possesses the following three

---

[22] At-Tawba 9:24

qualities will have the sweetness (delight) of faith: The one to whom Allah and His Apostle becomes dearer than anything else, Who loves a person and he loves him only for Allah's sake, Who hates to revert to (disbelief) as he hates to be thrown into the fire."

This is the case of sorcerers: when love dwells in their hearts, and they allowed sacrificing souls, and they say to Pharaoh, Judge whatever you want to judge[23], and when love is in the heart, all the senses will obey God, and this is the meaning of the divine talk that Al-Bukhari brought out in his Saheeh, and in it also, My slave continues coming nearer to Me is what I have enjoined upon him; and My slave keeps on coming closer to me through performing Nawafil (prayer or doing extra deeds

---

[23] This related to Quran verse in Surat Ta-Ha 20:65-73 " They said, "O Moses, either you throw or we will be the first to throw." (65) He said, "Rather, you throw." And suddenly their ropes and staffs seemed to him from their magic that they were moving [like snakes]. (66) And he sensed within himself apprehension, did Moses. (67) Allah said, "Fear not. Indeed, it is you who are superior. (68) And throw what is in your right hand; it will swallow up what they have crafted. What they have crafted is but the trick of a magician, and the magician will not succeed wherever he is." (69) So the magicians fell down in prostration. They said, "We have believed in the Lord of Aaron and Moses." (70) [Pharaoh] said, "You believed him before I gave you permission. Indeed, he is your leader who has taught you magic. So I will surely cut off your hands and your feet on opposite sides, and I will crucify you on the trunks of palm trees, and you will surely know which of us is more severe in [giving] punishment and more enduring." (71) They said, "Never will we prefer you over what has come to us of clear proofs and [over] He who created us. So decree whatever you are to decree. You can only decree for this worldly life. (72) Indeed, we have believed in our Lord that He may forgive us our sins and what you compelled us [to do] of magic. And Allah is better and more enduring." (73).

besides what is obligatory) till I love him. When I love him I become his hearing with which he hears, his seeing with which he sees, his hand with which he strikes, and his leg with which he walks;

It has been said that in some narrations, by me he hears, sees, strikes and walks. The real meaning is that the love of Allah, if it takes the heart and takes over it, then all the senses will do what satisfy God, and the soul will be calmed by the will of her God for its goal, and away from its desire. Oh, you worship Allah as he wants not as you want, as the one who worships as he want, he is like the one who worships Allah on an edge. If he is touched by good, he is reassured by it; but if he is struck by trial, he turns on his face [to the other direction]. He has lost [this] world and the Hereafter.

when the knowledge and love become more strong, their owner only wants what his master wants, and in some of the previous books, whoever loves Allah, then nothing to him will be more preferable than his satisfaction, and who loves the world, he will love his desire more than anything else.

Ibn Abi al-Dunya narrated from al-Hasan. He said: "I did not see with my eyes, speak with my tongue, nor did I strike with my hand, nor did I walk on my leg until I see the obedience of Allah or his disobedience. If it is obedience I do it, if it is disobedience I stop.

This is the case of the characteristics of true lovers, so you should understand, may Allah have mercy for you, this is one of the few mysteries of mystical unification (Tawhild). To this, the Prophet (peace and blessings of Allah be upon him) said in his sermon when he came to Madina: " love with all your hearts."[24] It was mentioned by Ibn Is'haq and others.

The one whose heart is filled with the love of Allah, there isn't anything more emptied than the self-desire and passion, and to this the talker pointed with his saying, "I have sealed my heart to love you alone, there will be no love but yours.... If I could close my eyes ... I will not see until I see you ... I love you not with my parts but with me as a whole ... and if your love is doesn't help me to move ... and in the loved ones, there is a specific one ... and another who claims to be partner with him ... if tears mixed in the cheeks ... it turns out who is really crying ... As for those who pretend crying, and the one who really cries will melt because of his love, and he will fall in desire the one who claims.

As long as there is something left for the lover for himself, nothing will be in his hand of love except claiming, but the true lover is the one who sacrifices for his beloved, with him he can hear and see.

The heart is the house of the Lord. In the Isra'iliyat[25], Allah says, I didn't fill my heaven or my earth, but the heart of my believer servant is filled with me.

---

[24] Lack Chain of Transmission

When the heart has something inside other than God, God is the most free from polytheism and does not accept the rivalry of idols, the truth is jealous of his believer servant to dwell in his heart other than Allah, or there is anything else that he doesn't like.... We wanted you spend when you blended ...

When the heart is filled with things other than Allah, God is richer rich than polytheism and does not accept the rivalry of idols of desires, he is jealous of his servant to dwell in his heart anything other than him, or there is in it anything that Allah doesn't like.

We wanted you as a whole but when you mixed, you become away the same amount that you are away from us.

We said to you, do not dwell in the heart other than us. You dwelled others, so you are not from us.

Tomorrow no one will survived except those who have met Allah with a sound heart nothing in it but Allah.

---

[25] Isra'iliyat is the stories or subject told by the Bani Israel in Sahih al-Bukhari Narrated Abu Huraira:
The people of the Scripture (Jews) used to recite the Torah in Hebrew and they used to explain it in Arabic to the Muslims. On that Allah's Messenger (ﷺ) said, "Do not believe the people of the Scripture or disbelieve them, but say: -- "We believe in Allah and what is revealed to us." And also it is important to note this Hadith which way the Author did mentioned here, in Sunan Abi Dawud Narrated AbuHurayrah:
The Prophet (ﷺ) said: relate traditions from the children of Isra'il; there is no harm.

Allah the most high said " يَوْمَ لَا يَنفَعُ مَالٌ وَلَا بَنُونَ إِلَّا مَنْ أَتَى اللَّهَ بِقَلْبٍ سَلِيمٍ "26 The Day when there will not benefit [anyone] wealth or children, But only one who comes to Allah with a sound heart."

The sound heart is the heart which is a pure one of sullying violations but the stained heart with abominable, it is not appropriate for being beside the Most Holy, only after He has purified himself in the purgatory of punishment, if he get rid of stain, then he can be appropriate to be near. "Allah the Almighty is good and accepts only that which is good.

But the sound hearts are fit to be near the beginning, " سَلَامٌ عَلَيْكُم بِمَا صَبَرْتُمْ فَنِعْمَ عُقْبَى الدَّارِ "Peace unto you for that ye persevered in patience! Now how excellent is the final home!" 27 " سَلَامٌ عَلَيْكُمْ طِبْتُمْ فَادْخُلُوهَا خَالِدِينَ "Peace be upon you! well have ye done! enter ye here, to dwell therein.28" الَّذِينَ تَتَوَفَّاهُمُ الْمَلَائِكَةُ طَيِّبِينَ يَقُولُونَ سَلَامٌ عَلَيْكُمُ ادْخُلُوا الْجَنَّةَ" The ones whom the angels take in death, [being] good and pure; [the angels] will say, "Peace be upon you. Enter Paradise.

Whoever does not burn his heart today with the fire of regret over what preceded or the fire of longing to meet the beloved, then the fire of the hell is hotter. The only one who needs to be purified is the one who did not complete the achievement of monotheism and the implementation of its rights

---

26 Ash-Shu'ara 26:88
27 Ar-Ra'd 13:24
28 Az-Zumar 39:73

The fire will be first enflamed for the monotheists slaves hypocrites their work and the first one is the scholar, and the fighter(Mojahed) and the one who gives charity just for showing off because the lesser shirk (polytheism) is showing-off (of good deeds)

The one who shows off doesn't look at the people with his knowledge but only because of his ignorance of the greatness of the Creator, he counterfeits the signature on the name of the king to take the bribes for himself and he purports that he is from the king's retinue, but he doesn't know the king at all.

The one who shows off inscribed the name of the king on the false dirham to be circulated and this is permissible only for the non-critic

And after the people of hypocrisy enters the fire, the owners of desires and the slaves of passions who obeyed their desire and disobeyed their master, but the true servants are told. " يَا أَيَّتُهَا

[T]29 "النَّفْسُ الْمُطْمَئِنَّةُ ارْجِعِي إِلَى رَبِّكِ رَاضِيَةً مَرْضِيَّةً فَادْخُلِي فِي عِبَادِي وَادْخُلِي جَنَّتِي

o

Lord, well-pleased and pleasing [to Him], And enter among My [righteous] servants, and enter My Paradise."

The hell is extinguished by the light of the faith of those who don't associate anything with Allah, it is mentioned in Hadith that the fire says to the believer, oh believer your light has extinguished my flame.[30]

---

[29] Al-Fajr 89: 27-30

In al-Musnad from Jabir from the Prophet (peace and blessings of Allah be upon him) said: all the righteous and fugitive will enter the hell, it will be peace as it was on Abraham, the fire has a noise from their cold, This is the legacy of the heirs of the devotees from the Intimate Friend of Allah (Ibrahim) peace be upon him[31], the hell is afraid of the of love in the hearts of lovers.

Al Junaid said, " the Fire said, O! Lord, if I did not obey you, would you punish me with something else more severe than me?" then he says that: I will punish you by my greatest punishment, it said: Is there any fire greater than me and more sever? He said: Yes, the fire of my love that lives in the hearts of my faithful believers.

Stop a little with it to me, nothing could be less than a sight. In the heart of lover, there is a great fire, the hottest hell is its coldest.

Without the tears of lovers that extinguishes some of the warmth of love, they will be burnt because of sorrow and sadness, ... Let him extinguish the fire with tears ... leave him leave, ask those who blame him to excuse him for a moment, with blaming not for longing he was killed.

---

[30] Note by Imam Al-Albani this Hadith is weak
[31] Refer to Al-Anbiya 21:68 – 69 "They said, "Burn him and support your gods - if you are to act." (68) Allah said, "O fire, be coolness and safety upon Abraham." (69)

Some of the knowledgeable say, "Is not it strange that I am between your eyes and in my heart, from longing to my Lord, like a flame that does not extinguish?"

I have not seen any fire like the fire of love... it increases as it is far from the stove, it doesn't extinguish.

Those who know do not have a duty without their masters and they don't have any worry about others. In the Hadith that who became worried about anything other than Allah, he is not from Allah[32].

Some of them say that whoever tells you that his parents have worry about other, do not believe him. Dawud Taie says your concern has distracted my worries, and prevented me from sleeping, my longing to see you prevented me from enjoying pleasant and was a barrier between me and desires I am needed in your prison, oh generous, I have no duty other than him, blaming me doesn't stop my love to him, what can I do if he frustrated and the hope was disappointed. I have no change with him

My brothers, if you understand this meaning, you understand the meaning of the words of the Prophet (peace and blessings of Allah be upon him) who testified that there is no God but Allah, believing this from his heart, Allah will make the Hell-Fire forbidden for him. but whoever enters the fire from the people

---

[32] Note by Imam Al-Albani this Hadith is so weak

of this word, it is just because that his belief has decreased in saying that. This word, if it is truly believed, it purifies the heart from all the things but except Allah, and if there is any remaining in the heart other than Allah, it is because of lack of honesty in saying it.

Whoever believed in saying that there is no God but Allah, he will not love anyone else other than Allah, and did not ask anyone else, did not fear anyone but Allah and rely only on Allah. And there will not be any remaining of his self-desire and passion. However, do not think that the lover is asked for preservation , but he is required whenever he can to avoid this stain

Zaid ibn Aslam said that Allah loves the slave until he reaches with his love for him to say go, do whatever you want, I have forgiven you. And Al Shabi said: "If Allah loves a slave, no sin will harm him. '

And the interpretation of this talk is that God Almighty has care of those who love him, so as long as this slave slipped in the gap of passion, he took his hand to the safe escape he makes repentance easy for him and alert him to the ugliness of the slip. And he will apologize quickly, and he will be tested by the calamities to be forgiven of what he has done

In some of the ancient books[33], Allah, the most high, says: The people who are remembering me , are the people who sit for me, the people of my obedience, the people of my dignity. The

---

[33] Maybe he meant the Isra'iliyat

people of my torment, I don't disappoint them from my mercy, if they repent, I am their lover, and if they do not repent, I am their doctor. I test them by misfortunes to cleanse them from mistakes.

In Sahih Muslim, reported by Jaber, that the prophet (peace and blessings be upon him) said: the fever cleanses out the sins in the same way that a furnace removes the dirt of iron."

In Al-Mosnad and Sahih Ibn Habbaan reported by Abdullah ibn Mughfil said that a man who met a woman who was a prostitute in the pre-Islamic period of ignorance and he flirted her until he extended his hand to her. She said, stop "Allah prevented shirk and brought Islam, so he left her and went away. He turned to look behind him until the wall hit his face, so he told the Prophet (peace and blessings of Allah be upon him) about that, he said: "You are the servant of Allah, and Allah wanted the good for you, and you are good. Then he said that if Allah wants something bad for his servant, he will hold his sin until he will be called to account on the Day of Resurrection.

O people, your hearts are originally purified, but it has been subjected to sprinkler of the unclean sins, so spray them with little tears of the eyes, and then it will be purified.

You must have the determination to weaning the souls from the breast of desire, as diet is the top of the medicine, when you feel like doing desire then say as the woman told that man who blooded his face, "Allah prevented shirk and brought Islam" , Islam requires surrender and obedience to ritual. Remind it for his praising in saying[34] " إِنَّ الَّذِينَ قَالُوا رَبُّنَا اللَّهُ ثُمَّ اسْتَقَمُوا " Indeed, those who have said, "Our Lord is Allah " and then remained on a right course

Let it know the monitoring of who is closer to it than jugular vein, so that it will be shy from his nearness and his looking. أَلَمْ إِنَّ رَبَّكَ لَبِالْمِرْصَادِ[35] "يَعْلم بِأَنَّ اللَّهَ يَرَى" Does he not know that Allah sees?[36] "" Indeed, your Lord is in observation.

A man seduced a woman in a desert at night, she refused, so he said to her, no one can see us except the planets; she said where is the one who made these planets.

A man tried hard to seduces a woman by force, and he ordered her to close the doors. He said to her: Is there a door that has not been closed? She said: yes, it is the door that is between us and Allah the most high, so he left her.

Some knowledgeable saw a man taking to a woman, he said verily Allah sees you, may Allah cover up your faults and hours.

Al Junaid was asked, what can help me to lower your gaze (on seeing what is illegal to look at), he said by knowing that Allah's sight is before yours. Al Mohasabi said that observation is the heart knows the closeness of the Lord, if the knowledge of Allah increases then shyness will be stronger because of his closeness and looking.

---

[34] Fussilat 41:30
[35] Al-Alaq 96:14
[36] Al-Fajr 89:14

The Prophet (peace and blessings of Allah be upon him) advised a man to be shy of Allah as he is shy of a good man from his clan, and his shyness does not leave him[37]. Some of them say that you should by shy from Allah as much as he is closed to you and fear from him as much as his ability on you. Some of them told me forty years ago that I have not walked any step not for Allah, and I do not look at anything I like because I feel shy from Allah Almighty ... As if you were watching me to take care of my thoughts... and another takes care of my sight and my tongue. I haven't seen any view after you, but I said they have forced me, I haven't heard anything away from you, I have never thought about anything except you, my heart feels only about you

---

[37] Note by Imam Al-Albani this Hadith is weak

CHAPTER 2

The benefits of There is no God but Allah.

The word of Tawheed (monotheism) has great virtues that cannot be explored here. Let us recall some of what is mentioned about it. It is the word of piety, as Umar (may Allah be pleased with him) said from the companions, it is the word of sincerity, the truth testifying, the call for truth and the innocence of shirk. For this reason, Allah created the creation. Allah Almighty said: "مَا خَلَقْتُ الْجِنَّ وَالْإِنسَ إِلَّا لِيَعْبُدُونِ"[38] " And I did not create the jinn and mankind except to worship Me. For this reason, the messengers were sent, and the books were revealed, as Allah the most high says: " وَمَا أَرْسَلْنَا مِن قَبْلِكَ مِن رَّسُولٍ إِلَّا نُوحِي إِلَيْهِ أَنَّهُ لَا إِلَٰهَ إِلَّا أَنَا فَاعْبُدُونِ"[39] And We sent not before you any messenger except that We revealed to him that, "There is no deity except

---

[38] Adh-Dhariyat 51:56
[39] Al-Anbiya 21:25

Me, so worship Me." Also Allah the most high says, " يُنَزِّلُ الْمَلَائِكَةَ He [40]"بِالرُّوحِ مِنْ أَمْرِهِ عَلَىٰ مَن يَشَاءُ مِنْ عِبَادِهِ أَنْ أَنذِرُوا أَنَّهُ لَا إِلَٰهَ إِلَّا أَنَا فَاتَّقُونِ sends down the angels, with the inspiration of His command, upon whom He wills of His servants, [telling them], "Warn that there is no deity except Me; so fear Me."

Allah mentioned the blessings for his slaves in the verse of the blessings of the so-called bees "Al Nahel", for this Ibn Ayina said that Allah hasn't granted a blessing for any slave better than letting them know that there is no God but Allah, and that there is no God but Allah to the people of Paradise is like the cold water for the people of the world. For this word, the Paradise (House of reward) and the hell (punishment) were prepared. And for it I ordered the messengers to fight, whoever says this word, he protects his money and blood, and who refuses it, his blood is shed.

It is the key to Paradise and the key for the call of messengers, by this word Allah called Moses in struggle.

In Musnad Albzar and other from Ayad Ansari from The Prophet (peace and blessings of Allah be upon him) said that : " surely , there is no God but Allah, is the word of truth, and it has a high rank to Allah, it is the word that whoever says it believing in it , he will enter the paradise, and who says it dishonestly, it will save his blood and money in the world and when he meets

---

[40] An-Nahl 16:2

his God, he will be called to account on the Day of Resurrection"[41]. It is the key to Paradise as mentioned before. And it is the price of paradise as Al-Hasan, and it from weak directions, and the one whose last word is this word, will enter the Paradise, and it deliverance from the fire. The Prophet (peace and blessings of Allah be upon him) heard the mu'adhdhin saying, 'I bear witness that there is no God but Allah." He said he is out of fire, In Sahih Muslim. and it makes forgiveness a must

In the Musnad by Shaddad ibn Aws and Obada Ibn al-Saamit that the Prophet (peace and blessings of Allah be upon him) said to his companions: "Lift up your hands and say, 'There is no God but Allah.' Then we raised our hands for an hour and then the Messenger of Allah put down his hand (peace and blessings be upon him) and he said: O! Allah all praise and gratitude belong to you for sending me with this word, and ordered me with it, and promised me Paradise as a reward for it, and you do not break your promise, then he informed the people of the good news that Allah has forgiven you,"[42] and this is the best of good

Abu Dhar said: 'O Messenger of Allah (or Muhammad), inform me about that takes me near to Paradise and draws me away from the Fire (of Hell). He (the messenger) said If you do a bad deed, do a good deed, because it is ten times. I said: O

---

[41] Note by Imam Al-Albani this Hadith is weak in Chain of Transmission
[42] Note by Imam Al-Albani this Hadith is weak in Chain of Transmission

Messenger of Allah, is there is no God but Allah from the good deeds. he said, it is the best of good deeds and it wipe out sins and errors.

In Sunan Ibn Majah from Umm Hanee from the Prophet (peace and blessings of Allah be upon him) he said: There is no God but Allah. Do not leave a sin and do not be preceded by any knowledge

Some salaf, was seen after his death in a dream. He was asked about his condition, he said: There is no God, but Allah has not left any sin and it renews the faith in the heart.

In Al-Musnad , that the Prophet (peace and blessings of Allah be upon him) said to his companions, "Renew your faith." They said: "How can we renew our faith?" he said: say "There is no God but Allah", nothing equals this word in its weight, if it is weighted with the heavens and earths, it will be greater,

As in Al Musnad about Abed Allah BinAmer, about the Prophet (peace and blessings of Allah be upon him) that Noah said to his son at the time of his death, I command you with there is no God but Allah, the seven heavens and the seven earths if they were placed in the hand and if there is no God but Allah was placed in the other hand, the hand that has there is no God but Allah will be greater.

If the seven heavens and the seven earths were in a circle, their talk will be, there is no God but Allah.

Also, It is narrated that 'Abd-Allaah ibn' Amer said that the Prophet (peace and blessings of Allah be upon him) said: That Musa (peace be upon him) said "O Lord, teach me something, that will remind me of you, and I will call you by, Allah said , 'O Musa,' say there is no God but Allah, he said there is no God but Allah , O Lord but I need something special for me, Allah said O Musa if the seven heavens and the seven earths are in one hand, and there is no god but Allah in the other hand. Then there is no God but Allah will be greater than them. [43]

Also, it is greater if it is weighted against the sins books, as in the Hadiths of records and card, it is narrated by Ahmad, An-Nasa'i

Also in the hadith of Abdullah bin Amer narrated the prophet (peace and blessings of Allah) be upon him, it is that which breaks blocking until it reaches God Almighty.

At-Tirmidhi In the hadeeth of 'Abd-Allaah ibn' Amr narrated he Prophet (peace and blessings of Allah be upon him) he said: there is no barrier between there is no God but Allah, and Allah till it reaches him.

It is also narrated by Abu Hurayrah the Prophet (peace and blessings of Allah be upon him) said: any servant says there is no God but Allah sincerely, the gates of heaven are opened for

---

[43] Note by Imam Al-Albani this Hadith is weak in Chain of Transmission

it, until it reaches to the throne, so long as he avoids the major sins.

It is narrated that Ibn 'Abbaas said that there is a barrier between everything and Allah except the saying that there is no God but Allah, as your lips do not conceal it, so that nothing will conceal it until it reaches Allah.

Abu Amamah said, any servant says there is no God but Allah sincerely, it will reach the throne, and Allah will look to him and accept his pray.

Al-Nasa'i reported in the Book of the Day and the Night from the hadith of two companions that the prophet (peace and blessings of Allah be upon him) said: whoever says: " there is no true god except Allah. He is One and He has no partner with Him. His is the sovereignty and His is the praise, and He is Omnipotent, sincerely from his soul believing it by his tongue, Allah will open the heaven for him and look at the one who says it on the earth, and it is the right for him to be given what he asked.

It is the word that Allah answers the one who says it, as reported by As al-Nasi, al-Tirmidhi and Ibn Hibbaan narrated from the hadith of Abu Hurayrah and Abu Sa'eed Prophet (peace and blessings of Allah be upon him) said: "If a person says: None has the right to be worshipped but Allah and Allah is the Most Great ,'Allah says: 'My slave has spoken the truth; there is none worthy of worship except I, and I am the Most Great.' If a person says: There is none worthy of worship except Allah alone), Allah says: 'My slave has spoken the truth; there is none worthy of worship except I, alone.' If he says, (There is none worthy of worship except Allah with no partner or associate),' Allah says: 'My slave has spoken the truth; there is none worthy of worship except I, with no partner or associate.' If he says: (There is none worthy of worship except Allah, all dominion is His and all praise is to Him),' Allah says: 'My slave has spoken the truth; there is none of worthy of worship except I, all dominion Mine and all praise is due to Me.' If he says: (There is none worthy of worship and there is no power and no strength except with Allah),' Allah says: 'My slave has spoken then truth; there is none worthy of worship except I, and there is no power and no strength except with Me.' He used to say "Whoever says it in his illness, then dies, the Fire shall not consume   him." and it is the best saying of the prophets.

"Whoever says it in his illness, then dies, the Fire shall not consume him." As stated in the du'aa 'on the day of' Arafah,

It is the best of remembrance as in Hadith of Jaber, that the 'The best of remembrance is (None has the right to be worshipped but Allah) , also it is reported by Ibn Abbas, The most beloved word to Allah is There is no God but Allah, he does not accept any action without this word. It is like freeing ten slaves and it is a protection against Satan.

In [Al-Bukhari and Muslim]. Abu Hurairah (May Allah be pleased with him) reported: "He who utters a hundred times in a day these words: He is One and He has no partner with Him; His is the sovereignty and His is the praise, and He is Omnipotent),' he will have a reward equivalent to that for emancipating ten slaves, a hundred good deeds will be recorded to his credit, a hundred of his sins will be blotted out from his scroll, and no one will exceed him in doing more excellent good deeds except someone who has recited these words more often than him.

In [Al-Bukhari and Muslim]. Abu Aiyub al-Ansari (May Allah be pleased with him) narrated, 'The Messenger of Allah (peace and blessings of Allah be upon him) said: "Whoever says it ten times: 'he will have a reward equivalent to that of emancipating four of the descendants of lsma'il from slavery.'"

And in Tirmidhi narrated bin Umar narrated, that :the Messenger of Allah (peace and blessings of Allah be upon him) said: "Whoever enters the marketplace and says: 'There is none worthy of worship except Allah, Alone, without partner, to Him belongs the dominion, and to Him is all the praise, He gives life and causes death, He is Living and does not die, in His Hand is the good, and He has power over all things, (' Allah shall record a million good deeds for him, wipe a million evil deeds away from him, and raise a million ranks for him." and in another narration that a house will be built for him in the Paradise.

Among other its virtues of this word is that it is a safe from the grave's solitude and the fear of gathering, as in al-Musnad and others, narrated the Prophet (peace and blessings of Allah be upon him) said: " Those who say There is no God but Allah have no solitude in their graves and in their resurrection, The people of there is no God but Allah if they stand up from their graves, they shook the dust that is on their heads and say, "Praise be to Allah, who has gone away sorrow and grieve from us." [44]

In a hadeeth mursal i.e., a successor narrated it directly from the Prophet (peace and blessing be upon him), he said: whoever says "There is no God but Allah, the King , the Truth , the Manifest , a hundred time every day, it will be safe and protection from poverty, and affability from grave's solitude, and it will brought richness for him and open the door of paradise for him.

It is the motto of believers if they stand from their graves, Al-Nadar ibn Arabi said that I have been told that if people came out from their graves, their motto will be there is no God but Allah

Al-Tabaraani has recently stated in Hadith Marfu' that the motto of this nation on the Sirat (that is, the Bridge set over Hell-fire) is that there is no God but you.[45]

One of its virtues is that it opens the door of the eight gates of Paradise for the one who says it, so he can enter the Paradise from any door that he likes.

As in the hadeeth of 'Umar narrated the Prophet (peace and blessings of Allah be upon him) for those who testify the two Testification after Wudu In [Al-Bukhari and Muslim].

Narrated by Ibn al-Saamit (may Allah be pleased with him) said that the Prophet (peace and blessings of Allah be upon him) said:

"He who bears witness that there is no true god except Allah, alone having no partner with Him, that Muhammad is His slave

---

[44] It is not in Musnad Ahmad and Note by Imam Al-Albani the Hadith is weak
[45] Note by Imam Al-Albani this Hadith as weak

and His Messenger, that 'Isa (Jesus) is His slave and Messenger and he (Jesus) is His Word which He communicated to Maryam (Mary) and His spirit which He sent to her, that Jannah is true and Hell is true; Allah will make him enter Jannah from the eight doors from any door he likes.

In the hadeeth of 'Abd al-Rahmaan ibn Samra narrated that the Prophet (peace and blessings of Allah be upon him) in a story of his long sleep and he said, "I saw a man from my nation ending up in the gates of Paradise. The doors were closed for him, then the testifying that there is no God but Allah came to him, it opened the doors for him and brought him to Paradise[46]

One of its virtues is that its people if they entered the fire by not doing its rights perfectly, they must come out of it.

In Sahih Bukhari and Sahih Muslim the prophet (peace and blessings of Allah be upon him) he said: " Then Allah will say, 'By my Power, and my Majesty, and by My Supremacy, and by My Greatness, I will take out of Hell (Fire) whoever said: 'None has the right to be worshipped except Allah."

Al-Tabaraani narrated that Anas narrated that the Prophet (peace and blessings of Allah be upon him) said: "Some people of no god but Allah enter the Fire because of their sins, the worshipers of al-Lat and al-'Uzza tell them, the saying that there is no God but Allah hasn't benefited you, so Allah will be angry and He will bring them out of the Fire, and they will enter Paradise.

---

[46] Note by Imam Al-Albani this Hadith as weak

The one who is kind in his anger, so how can he be if he is satisfied ? he doesn't make equal those who believe in his oneness even though they are not perfect in the rights of his monotheism and between those who made partner to him.

Some of the salaf said that Ibrahim (peace be upon him) says" O Allah, don't associate those who associating with you anything and those who don't associate anything to you"

Some of the salaf said in their prayer, O Allah, that you said about the people of Hell that they and they swore their strongest oaths by Allah the who will die will not be raised. And we swear with our strongest oaths that Allah will raise out anyone who dies, don't associate the two parties in the same house.

Abu Sulaiman was saying that if he asked me for my stint, I will ask him for his generosity, if he asked me for my sins I will ask him for his forgiveness, even though he put me in fire I will tell the people of the fire that I love him.

What a beautiful and nice to be linked to him, what a difficult to leave him, in anger and satisfaction what admirable he is, the heart loves him even though he is punished.

Some of those who knew were crying all night long and say that you if torment me, I love you and if you grant me mercy, I love you.

The knowledgeable are afraid of the veil more than they fear of torment. Tha Al Noon said the fear of the fire at the time of separation is like a drop in an unfathomable sea, some of them say my God and master, if you tortured me with all your punishment, what I missed from your closeness was greater than torment, some of them were asked if he expelled you, what will you do?

If I didn't find contact from love …. I will be in fire … I will annoy its people with my call…in all its spaces in the morning and in the evening. People of Quraish cried a lot on the one who claims that he loves the Glorious … and he was dishonest in his claiming, so he will be punished the severe punishment

My brothers, work hard today to achieve monotheism, no one will be saved from Allah's punishment except those who say there is no God but Allah.

No one will say anything better than saying that there is no God but Allah, Glory be to God Almighty and who …. I pear that there is no God but him …. who can forgive my sins … O Allah, other than you …. O there is no God but him …. Paradises of Immortality for those believe in his monotheism… I witness that there is no God but him …. His fire doesn't burn who …. witnesses that there is no God but him …. I say it sincerely without scrimp, I pear that there is no God but Allah.

ABOUT THE AUTHOR

Imam Ibn Rajab al Hanbali (736 - 795 AH)

He was born in Baghdad in 736H and was raised by a knowledgeable family, firmly rooted in knowledge, nobility and righteousness. His father played the greatest role in directing him towards the beneficial knowledge.

Al-Haafidh Ibn Rajab, may Allaah have mercy on him, was deeply attached to the works of Shaikh-ul-Islaam Ibn Taimiyyah, for he would issue legal rulings according to them and would constantly reference his books. This is since he served as a student under Ibn Qayyim al-Jawziyyah, the most outstanding student of Shaikh-ul-Islaam Ibn Taimiyyah, may Allah have mercy on all of them. But in spite of this, he (rahimahullaah) wasn't a blind follower or a fanatical adherent (to his teacher). Rather, he would review, authenticate, verify and follow the evidences.

Al-Haafidh Ibn Rajab, may Allaah have mercy on him passed to the realm of the Akhira in Ramadaan, 795H. He died while in Damascus.

www.ingramcontent.com/pod-product-compliance
Lightning Source LLC
Chambersburg PA
CBHW030305030426
42337CB00012B/589